The Fear Course Guide:

How to do Job Interviews Without the Nerves

How to do Job Interviews Without the Nerves

By David J. Wilkinson
The Fear Course

Visit: http://www.fearcourse.com

This document is copyright 2010 © David J Wilkinson. All rights reserved. None of this document or any parts of the document, content or design may be copied by any means whatsoever or distributed without express written permission of the author.

ISBN 978-1-4461-5838-8

How to do a Job Interview without the Nerves

Contents:

Introduction

Introduction 5
Some Research 6
In this guide 7
Two types of people 8
About this guide 9

About your nerves

Some stuff about your nerves 11
What happens when we get scared or nervous? 12
Clever stuff (FCC) 13
Not so clever stuff (FCC) 14
Polarization 16
Is it real ? 17
Where does our fear come from? 19
F.E.A.R. 21
Other things that feel like fear 22
Correct diet to help reduce anxiety 23

Techniques

The balance 26
Rebalancing 28
Mind your Language 30
Mind, body and our emotions 36
Looking 38
Breathing 39
How to Chill 41
Dealing with panic 42
A great strategy for dealing with panic attack 45
The Balcony Technique 46
Let the music play 48
Mental Movies 49

Plans

A plan for the day of the interview 51
A Plan for the interview 52

References 56

Introduction

How to do a Job Interview without the Nerves

Introduction

So you are going to have a job interview soon. Congratulations! I know you might be nervous or anxious about this now, but let's celebrate the success you have already had by getting an interview. Just getting interview is an achievement in itself. We now need to get you calm, and composed for the interview so that you can perform well. Now I can not guarantee you will get the job, that depends on a whole host of factors like qualifications, experience, fit of your abilities to those required by the employer and so on, however we can help you to become a whole lot calmer and more composed during the interview.

This book also has video and audio tutorials and exercises associated with it. Go to

http://www.fearcourse.com/index.php?option=com_content&view=article&id=279

and signup right now to get access to them FREE.

If you would like one-to-one support and even more techniques why don't you try the **Online Fear Course**?

You will get :

- ➤ The **entire one day live course** in text, audio and video worth $265
    - o 5 Stages, and
    - o 29 Individual Step-by-Step Tutorials
    - o 7 Major Pathways, including
        - Presentation nerves worth $169
        - Driving test nerves worth $54
        - Fear of flying worth $169
        - Social & dating nerves worth $99
        - Job interview nerves worth $169
        - Download handouts worth $25
        - Online support via online forum $75
        - Voucher for the live fear course $50
        - One Year 'Confidence Course' $80
    - o Full support via the VIP forum $200
    - o One year Confident Habits Course $175

Go to www.fearcourse.com/ and click 'online'.

Some research

We recently conducted a survey about job interview nerves and discovered that:

- 93% of people suffer from some form of nerves at some stage before or during the interview.
- A very small percentage of those, about 2%, have panic attacks at some point.
- About 11% of people fail to turn up for the interview because of nerves
- Of those that do turn up 8% freeze during the interview and can't speak
- 43% get their words mixed up or don't say what they what they want to because of the nerves
- 12% say the nerves helped them perform better during the interview
- 77% state they performed worse than they knew they could do had it not been for their nerves.

It doesn't have to be like this. Just about anyone can reduce or even kill their nerves completely and I am going to show you how in this special guide.

How to do a Job Interview without the Nerves

In this guide

In this guide I will show you how to deal with all of your nerves, anxieties and even panic attacks.

Have you noticed how when you are nervous, not only do you not enjoy things as much as you do when you are nice and relaxed but also things like your sense of humour tend to disappear as well?

When people are nervous or even get into a panic a number of things happen to them that don't happen to calm and composed people. For example nervous people tend to:

- Make worse decisions,
- Get brain fade and not be able to think straight or remember things as well,
- Enjoy things less,
- Get into more of a negative mindset and can,
- Catastrophes – see disasters where there are non, this is the ability to turn molehills into mountains,
- Generally perform less well, and
- Have problems remembering things correctly
- Lack emotional control.
- As well as that it just doesn't feel as good as being calm and happy!

How to do a Job Interview without the Nerves

Two types of people

This guide will show you how to achieve calm on the run up to and during your interview; how to be relaxed and composed so that you can perform as well as you know you can.

People who have learnt to be calm and composed in such situations tend to:

1. Firstly calm people come over better to the interviewers, who would you want to hire, a bag of nerves or a calm confident person?
2. Secondly they perform better on the day in that they can remember things and answer questions more confidently and fluently. Also if they don't now something are far less likely to get flustered and would have the confidence to be hoes say they don't know.
3. Lastly they make better decisions.

You can easily be like either type of person, stressed, nervous and prone to panic OR calm, composed, in control and prone to enjoying themselves. You can't be both anxious and relaxed at the same time.

This guide shows you how to be the latter. If this is what you want to be like then read on.

How to do a Job Interview without the Nerves

About this guide:

Throughout this guide you will find places to make notes of things and to note down your answers to stuff.

This guide has 4 sections:

Introduction – This bit

About your nerves This is important and will show you what is happening to you. Whilst it is tempting to just go on to the techniques you will find that this section will help a lot.

Techniques. This section will get you into the habit of calm before the day. Like all habits they take a little time to get into. The preparation you do here is worth its weight in gold.

Plans. You should use these on the day and during the run up to your interview. They will guide you through the process.

Ok so let's get going:

How to do a Job Interview without the Nerves

About your nerves

How to do a Job Interview without the Nerves

About your nerves

The first thing you need to know about nervousness is that it is a level of fear, as are anxiety and worry.
I just want you to think about these for a moment. If you were to put the following in order of severity for you, what order would you put them in? (1 - 5, 1 being the most severe and 5 being least severe for you).

Nervousness	1
Worry	4
Fear	3
Anxiety	2
Panic	5

Whilst anxiety, worry, nervousness and fear are different levels of fear, panic and panic attacks in particular are somewhat different.

How to do a Job Interview without the Nerves

What happens when we get scared or nervous?

When we get scared there is a small bit of our brain that takes control of us. In essence this bit (called the Amygdala if you must know) is like a Fear Command Centre right in the centre of our brains.

There are a few things you should know about your Fear Command Centre (FCC).

1. It is very old. Way older than you are. Approximately 208 million years older than you are actually.
2. The F.C.C. evolved in order to stop all the first mammals being eaten by the much older (and bigger) reptiles and dinosaurs which have a couple of things in common:
    a. They tend to be big
    b. They tend to have big appetites
    c. They usually have very big teeth
    d. They attack first and burp afterwards – they don't ask questions.
3. The ability to get a warm meal in the form of a nice cruchy mammal didn't do a lot for the furry ones. In fact until fear made an appearance, the half-time score was not looking good. As it turned out, attacking great big green things that have sharp teeth and tough scales was not a great survival strategy. So the FCC evolved and gave us some other options:
    a. Run away and hide. This works a treat if the big green scary thing isn't too close. As a little diversion the FCC also gets you to leave a smelly pile in the hope that any chasing dinosaur will sniff that rather than continuing the chase, which is why scared people often feel the need to go to the toilet.
    b. Freeze. If you are too close, running won't work as you are likely to be caught. Now, as most predators require things

to move to be able to see them, so freezing isn't a bad strategy.
c. Finally, if none of these work fight back.

How to do a Job Interview without the Nerves

Clever stuff

The Amygdala (FCC) is a really clever and really dim bit of kit all at the same time.

The clever things it does:

1. It scans everything for a threat of being eaten.
2. If it thinks you are in danger of being eaten it:
    a. Makes you want to run away if the danger isn't too close
    b. Makes you want to go to the toilet as a diversion to any chasing reptiles
    c. Starts to focus (narrow) your vision so you don't get distracted from the task of running away
    d. Shuts down your hearing so you don't get distracted by the roaring behind you
    e. Numbs your feelings so you don't get distracted by scratches as you run
    f. Closed your blood vessels, so if you cut yourself as you run you don't leave a nice trail for the predator to follow
    g. Stops you thinking so you concentrate on running and not going "Oh look what big eyes you have". Also thinking is slow and it needs you to move fast so thinking is a hindrance.
3. If the danger is too close it:
    a. Shuts everything down so you freeze in the hope the predator will find something more interesting to do

How to do a Job Interview without the Nerves

Not so clever stuff

The FCC is a really old bit of equipment that hasn't had any updates in millions of years.

The dim things the FCC does:

1. All the FCC does is looking for something scary. Nothing else.
2. It errs on the side of caution. But there again wouldn't you be if being eaten was a distinct possibility?
3. It thinks everything that is scary, is scary because it will eat you and you will die. Jobs and interviews hadn't been invented when the Fear Control Centre was first opened.
4. Our imaginations also hadn't been invented back then. The FCC thinks anything you imagine is real.
5. The clock is broken in the Fear Control Centre. The only time is NOW. There is no future.
6. If you think of (imagine) something scary it thinks it must be real, it will eat you and you will die, right now.

So it leaps into action to save you from being eaten. It starts you feeling like you want to run away the moment you think of doing your speech or getting married. Now, it may have escaped your notice but in my experience not many people get eaten during a job interview.

So the FCC - neat and clever if you are being hunted, but not so wonderful if all you want to do is sparkle at an interview.

How to do a Job Interview without the Nerves

What would you do if you won the lottery?

What would you do if you if you won the lottery?

My guess is your answer might include all or some of the following:

- Big house
- New car(s)
- Holiday
- Give some to:
    - Family
    - Charity
- Go shopping...And more.

Or did you say that you would buy something like a packet of sweets? No? Odd that most people just think about winning 'the big one' when asked that question.

Have you ever looked forward to something, the anticipation of which turned out to be better than the actual event?

Have you ever been nervous about doing something before the event, and then once you have done it, wonder what you were nervous about?

This is called Polarization.

How to do a Job Interview without the Nerves

Polarization

Polarization is our ability to polarize our thoughts; to make leaps of imagination. We tend to do this most when we are either very optimistic about something or very pessimistic.

A recent study asked new business owners for their projections for their business for the first three years. They found that:

- 100% of the projections were positive
- That each year was incremental, every year the business would get better
- They would have a fully fledged business within 3 years

80% of businesses fail in the first three years.

This is a nice (but sad) example of polarization at work.

When we are nervous about something we also polarize our thoughts and make negative extrapolations, which are usually worst-case scenarios. These are just our imagination making free with our fears.

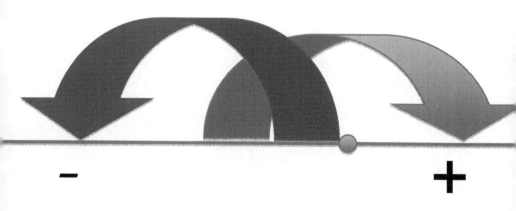

How to do a Job Interview without the Nerves

Is it real?

A few years ago, I did some research looking the fear of job interviews. A month before their interview I asked people what they were worried about. These were the results, in order of frequency the top four fears were:

1. Freezing up during the interview
2. Falling over / feinting
3. Forgetting what they want to say
4. Doing / saying something stupid

I then asked the people if they have ever either

a. Had this happen to them before, or
b. Seen it happen to anyone else.

Less than 0.03% answered yes. 0.03 percent of people questioned had any of the top four fears occur to them, and

0.05 percent or less than 1 in a 1000 had seen it happen to anyone else. Your odds of having a car crash are bigger!

And yet the fear grips us.

Where does our fear come from?

Some other research I was involved in; looked at what activated people's fears.

We found that there were two main types of fear activation:

1. Episodic or fear from a remembered source. In other words fear that has developed because of a real past experience.
2. Imagination, or fear we construct that isn't part of a memory of a real event. This is a constructed fear.

We had people keep diaries over a 6 month period of their fears and anxieties and then interviewed them to find out what category their fears fell into.

Any guesses what we found?

How to do a Job Interview without the Nerves

On average about 7% of peoples day-to-day fears are as a result of something that had actually happened to them in the past.

The rest (93%) were imagined!

We then found something else.

There imagined fears split into two types:

1. Evidenced based, and
2. Imagination

Evidenced based imagined fears (things that hadn't happened to them) are those fears where there is some evidence in the situation that what is feared will occur. An example would be getting on board an aeroplane where the wing was loose or hanging off!

Imagination based fears are those situations where there is no evidence in the situation to suggest the fear will be realised, for example getting on a perfectly serviceable, new aeroplane.

You have to admit that not many people die from doing an interview. The risk level is actually quite minimal, unfortunately our brain, or at least part of our brain defaults to protecting us from being eaten. It developed at a time when ending up as a sabre-toothed tiger's lunch was a little more likely than messing up at a job interview and hasn't really grown up since.

F.E.A.R.

As a result of the research you have just seen and your own experiences of episodic and anticipatory fears there is an acronym for fear, which I use when, I start to feel nervous or anxious about doing something. I find it helps in situations of low anxiety and nerves, when I remember that fear is just:

F - False

E - Evidence

A - Appearing

R - Real

So not only do we have some very old and very simple equipment driving us, but we have added an imagination to make the scary things even bigger, more scary and appear to us like they are absolutely everywhere; under the bed, in cupboards - there is no limit to our imagination. Not too useful when we are faced with a job interview.

How to do a Job Interview without the Nerves

There are a couple of things that feel like fear but ...

There are number of medical and medically related issues that can imitate the symptoms of fear, anxiety or nervousness. If you find that your symptoms persists it might be an idea to seek medical advice.

a. Hypoglycaemia - Eating junk and sweet food can cause the blood sugar levels to fall too low, which in turn can bring about a variety of symptoms that are similar to panic attacks - anxiety, feeling shaky, weakness etc.

b. An over-active thyroid can cause a rapid heartbeat, sweats, and the sensation of anxiety.

c. Heart complaints - some heart complaints can mimic the symptoms of anxiety and even panic.

d. Hormonal imbalances - again a number of hormonal problems can create panic attack and anxiety like symptoms.

e. IBS or Irritable Bowel Syndrome - whilst it is thought that IBS may be brought on by stress, some of the symptoms of IBS are often very similar to those of anxiety, nervousness and sometimes fear.

f. Drugs - a number of legal and illegal drugs like caffeine, nicotine, marijuana, cocaine and others can create or have side or after effects of panic, nervousness and anxiety.

g. Nutrients - it is also believed that the lack of certain nutrients such as vitamins B and C can also add to anxiety problems.

Each of the above can lead to symptoms almost indistinguishable from fear, panic, nervousness or anxiety. If you can't find another trigger or you think that you may be at risk from any of the above you should seek medical advice.

Eating our way to anxiety – 6 rules to avoid it:

Some foods contribute to anxiety and some aid calmer dispositions.

There are 6 golden rules with diet that help to reduce anxiety and increase calmer states:

(1) Eat plenty on complex carbohydrates such as lots of fresh fruit and whole grain foods. These can act as tranquilisers by increasing serotonin levels in the brain.

(2) Most type of milk and if you eat meat, turkey increases levels of tryptophan, which is a precursor to serotonin. Again these have been linked to good mental health.

(3) Keep well hydrated with water. Dehydration can create the feelings of anxiety, so drinking plenty of water helps reduce this side effect.

(4) High levels of caffeine can cause jittery feelings and increased levels of anxiety, so reducing caffeine laden drinks like coffee and fizzy drinks will help a lot.

(5) Frequent small meals can keep blood sugar levels even rather than two or three large meals a day which cause peaks and troughs in blood sugar levels both of which can cause feelings of anxiety.

(6) Reduce sugary and high salt foodstuffs like sweets, crisps, puddings etc. Again these can cause anxiety like symptoms.

Look at your diet over the last week, what have you consumed?

Make sure that on the morning of the interview you eat and have some fruit (not sugary sweets) close by to nibble on during the day and have plenty of water. It's a good idea to carry some fruit either fresh or dried and a bottle of water for you during the day. Obviously you don't want to be eating and drinking during the interview, that would be more than a little odd.

The number one reason for feinting at an interview is lack of food and water.

A really good breakfast on the morning of your interview would be porridge, fruit and yoghurt.

How to do a Job Interview without the Nerves

Techniques

The balance:

Imagine a balance:

Poof! One balance…

Now imagine that on one side of the balance is your thinking and on the other side of the balance are your emotions and feelings.

Sometimes you will find that you have been concentrating on something so much that you don't notice time flying. When I am writing articles and things like this book for instance I often find that I have been concentrating so hard that when I 'come round' my legs won't work, it has gone dark and I realise I haven't eaten all day.

I am sure that there will have been times when you have been feeling nervous or sad or something similar and then something happens that you have to focus on. Did you notice what happens to those feelings? They subside right?

Then when you realise the feelings have subsided what happens?

Yup, they come back.

Then when we are anxious, have you noticed the more anxious you get the harder it is to think straight? If you have ever got into a total panic (a blind panic) about something, you may have noticed that you can't think at all.

- As anxiety rises our ability to think decreases
- As we focus more and more on something our anxieties reduce.

Now that's not just interesting, it's useful.

Rebalancing

This is the start of the techniques to help you become calm and composed, and stay that way, no matter what. We want you to ace your wedding and your speech. Read on...

The trick here is to take control of the balance so you can swing it in your favour as and when you decide. Not only that I am about to show you how to do it in seconds and all without the aid of stabilisers.

Emotional Resilience.

Contrary to popular belief emotional resilience is not about not feeling things - that is called being dead. Emotional Resilience is Emotional Intelligence or the ability to know what you (and others) are feeling + the ability to be able to control your emotions at will, rather than the other way around. So if you are feeling nervous about something an emotionally resilient person can deal with the emotions in a positive way and not let their emotions affect their performance.

Back to rebalancing:

There are three principles that make rebalancing work

1. It is very difficult to focus on two things at the same time.
2. It's easier to increase something than reduce or stop something. What I mean by this is that it is easier to concentrate on increasing thinking rather than trying to concentrate on reducing our emotions.
3. You can't be both relaxed and anxious at the same time! If you are anxious you can't be relaxed and if you are relaxed you can't be anxious. Try it you will see what I mean.

Following these three principles helps us to construct a series of powerful rebalancing techniques:

The first rebalancing technique is a very simple one. This works for low-grade nerves and stops them becoming whopping big panics. It is called The Focussed Distraction Technique.

You will no doubt have noticed when you are anxious that if you end up having to focus on something else, some form of distraction, the nerves will subside or even go away. The easiest method then is to do something, anything that you have to concentrate and focus on outside of you. A sport, a game, puzzles, work, a pastime, counting backwards from 100, absolutely anything that you have to focus on. The best things to concentrate on are things that are meaningful and require your attention to do them.

There is a video for you to watch Go to video 1 now. If you haven't already done so sign up at http://www.fearcourse.com/ to get the video and audio files.

How to do a Job Interview without the Nerves

The second rebalancing technique is really nice and normally calms people within a few moments. Positive Imagery works really well when you are nervous and it has the added bonus of putting you in a good place.

Think about a really pleasant past experience and make the image as real as possible. Concentrate on the detail, every detail and build a real picture.

a) What was the weather like?

b) Who was there?

c) What was said?

d) What order did things happen in?

e) What were people wearing?

f) Imagine the sensation of the sun or the rain of the day or the sand under your feet, or whatever.

Find yourself a quite spot relax and Listen here

The last rebalancing technique will really chill you out. Again find a quiet spot to yourself for a couple of minutes and go to the second link in the email you were sent to really relax.

How to do a Job Interview without the Nerves

Mind your Language

The language that we use when we talk and the language we use when we think has a great impact on how we feel. Our language and thinking can contribute a lot to feeling of anxiety. I am about to read out six sentences. I will do this four times and on each reading I will change the sentence a little. See what difference it makes for you. Look at the following messages that people often tell themselves and others:

a. I know I will feel terrible when I go out/do this.

b. I can't do it.

c. I always have to have a drink before I can do this.

d. It's not safe.

e. It will all go wrong.

f. It's a disaster.

Listen to the third audio file linked in the email you were sent.

I want you to actually say these sentences out loud and notice how you feel as you say them.

These are called negative certainties. They are negative and ...

How to do a Job Interview without the Nerves

Now read these out loud: or listen to the link you were sent for this page.

1. I might feel terrible when I go out/do this.
2. I might not be able to do it
3. I might have to have a drink before I can do it
4. It might not be safe
5. It could all go wrong
6. It could be a disaster

Notice a difference?

These are called negative possibilities. They are negative things to say but they also allow the possibility that something else might happen.

How to do a Job Interview without the Nerves

Now try these... or to the audio files linked to this page in the email you were sent.

1. I might feel OK when I go out/do this.
2. I might be able to do it
3. I might not have a drink before I can do it this time
4. It might be safe
5. It could all go OK
6. It could be OK

How did that feel? These are called positive possibilities. They are largely positive sentences that have a possibility that something else might happen. The important thing here is that they make you feel like you can achieve and do what you want. This is a world of difference from what negative certainties do to us.

How to do a Job Interview without the Nerves

Lastly try saying these out loud:

1. I Can do this and feel good
2. I can do it
3. I can just do it, I don't need anything else.
4. It will be safe; I will make sure it is safe.
5. It will be good.
6. It will work; I will make sure it does.

You can listen to by clicking on the link for this page in the email you have been sent.

Now this feels a whole lot different doesn't it? It feels empowering and 'can do' as opposed to limiting and fear riddled.

You have control of the language you use with yourself and others.

It makes a big difference to how we feel. Use it.

How to do a Job Interview without the Nerves

What messages do you hear from others or do you give to yourself that are similar?

Positive thinking depends on positive language. Notice that a lot of the words being used above are very definite and rigid, e.g. will, have to, always, can't - these words encourage us to look negatively at a situation and do not allow for any hope or possibility of change.

Suggestions: Avoid always, ever, must, should, have to, never, and can't etc.

Try: maybe, possibility, hopefully, sometimes, perhaps etc.

Your thinking plays an important part in keeping anxiety going or even making it worse. Change your thinking – change your emotional state.

If you find yourself thinking or even saying "I am going to be really nervous." Guess what will happen.

If you start to feel nervous at any stage, rather than thinking or saying "I feel nervous" say

"I am feeling calmer and calmer".

Notice what happens.

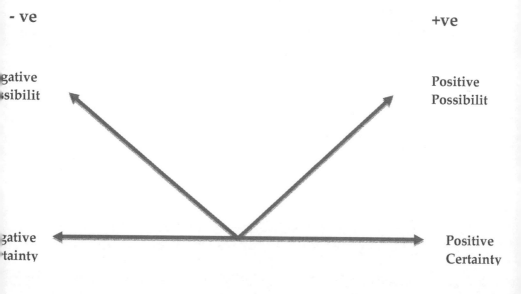

How to do a Job Interview without the Nerves

Mind, body and our emotions:

Think about this. How would you know if someone is anxious?

What does their face look like?

What do they do with their eyes?

How do they hold their body?

What are their actions like?

Now what I want you to do is take on all of these traits and notice what happens.

Feeling nervous eh?

Yes our body language and our emotions are intimately linked.

How to do a Job Interview without the Nerves

Ok so try this:

Sit or stand up straight,

Lift your chin slightly

Look up slightly

Pull your shoulders back

If you are standing, stand with your legs slightly apart

Look confident – what happens?

Yep you feel confident. Use this.

How to do a Job Interview without the Nerves

Looking

I want you to sit or stand still. Keep your head straight and then look down, moving only your eyes. Notice what happens to your energy.

Notice what happens to how you feel as you keep looking down.

Now, without moving your head look up slightly above the horizon. Notice what happens to your energy and feelings.

Most people find that their energy moves up and they feel lighter or more confident. This is very important when you get married or give your speech. Looking up can make a big difference to how you feel.

Breathing - it helps.

The second most frequent cause of feinting (after a lack of food and water) at wedding ceremonies and receptions is a lack of breathing control. You may have noticed what happens when we get anxious or stressed. We tend to breathe more shallowly. What this does is not allow the oxygen and carbon dioxide to exchange properly in your lungs and the carbon dioxide levels in our bloodstream increases. Some of the side effects of high carbon dioxide in our blood are similar to the feelings of anxiety.

There are few simple breathing techniques that can quickly reduce negative feelings such as anxiety, fear even anger and help you to relax quickly - within seconds.

There are two principles for breathing:

1. Shallow breathing creates imbalances between oxygen and carbon dioxide in the blood stream, which in turn promotes feeling of anxiety as well as other problems

2. Deep breathing maintains balance within the bloodstream, and induces states of relaxation.

Breathing techniques work like this on fear:

* If you change your thinking - your breathing will get deeper and slower

* Change your breathing - your thinking will get calmer and clearer

Diaphramatic breathing

Instructions for part one

1. Stand or sit up straight
2. Pull back your shoulders
3. Breath in slowly through your nose whilst counting slowly up to 5 and pushing your stomach out.
4. Hold the breath for a count of 2
5. Breathe out through your mouth whilst counting slowly to down to 1 from 5 and pulling your stomach in.
6. The online fear course gives you even more powerful breathing techniques, including instructional videos and support.

This time whilst you are breathing in through your nose and pushing your stomach out imagine you are breathing in energy and that it is spreading throughout your body.

As you hold your breath with your lungs full, imagine the energy growing in intensity.

When you exhale through your mouth feel all the tension and anxiety leaving with the exhaled air, let it go.

How to Chill

This section of the course has been designed to help you to relax anywhere at any time. There are techniques you can use without anyone knowing.

Each audio file is a different relaxation technique and you can download them without the preamble from the resource area, so that you can take them anywhere.

Now sit back, and use the **four** links included in your email for this page, listen and relax ...

Dealing with panic

Panic Attacks:

Panic attacks are a little different from anxiety and fear issues. Unlike fear and anxiety panic attacks are often not associated with an incident as such. There is also a fair amount of research evidence to show that they have slightly different pathways in the brain. Panic attacks tend to happen unpredictably and unconnected to anything else.

Anyone can get them but...

It is estimated that approximately 15% of people experience panic attacks at some time in their life. The most common age of onset is the mid-teens and early adulthood. However, panic attacks may begin at any time, with the maximum risk of panic attacks being between the ages of 25 and 44 years. Women are between 2 - 3 times more likely to suffer from panic attacks as men. People who live on their own or are not in a stable relationship, not working and have lower educational attainment tend to suffer more than others.

However... anyone can get them.

Symptoms

Panic attacks are characterised by sudden and unexpected distinct period of intense fear, nervousness or apprehension, terror, panic or discomfort. They are often accompanied by physical symptoms, such as shortness of breath, dizziness, palpitations, heart pain, excessive perspiration, trembling, nausea or abdominal distress; and cognitive symptoms such as depersonalisation or derealisation, and the fear of losing control, going crazy, having a heart attack, or even dying.

The first things to realise are that

- A panic attack cannot cause your heart to stop.
- A panic attack cannot cause you to stop breathing.
- A panic attack cannot cause you to go crazy and lose mental control.
- Panic attacks come quickly and then go. They are always temporary.

How to do a Job Interview without the Nerves

The problem:

Due to the unpredictable nature of panic attacks people can often build up quite a fear of them. This often prompts the person to engage in severe avoidance behaviour of various types. Additionally panic attacks can knock the confidence and lower the individuals self esteem.

How to do a Job Interview without the Nerves

A great strategy for dealing with panic attack

1. There is a general principle; if you can observe something it can't be you. Realise this: You are not your emotions. You are not your thoughts. The more you learn to 'observe' – notice and identify your emotions the less of a hold they will have on you.

2. A panic attack is like a flood. It happens outside of you, but you can get caught up in it. The thing about floods is that they are temporary. Floods come quickly and they then subside just like a panic attack. They may be unexpected but they are only temporary. The waters rise quickly and then flow away.

3. What happens if you battle against a flood? You end up weakening yourself and making things very difficult. It's the same with panic attacks. The more you fight the harder they appear to be. The big difference between a flood and a panic attack is that you cannot really drown or even get wet.

You will not run out of breath, you will not have a heart attack and you will not, cannot die from a panic attack, and it will pass. So you are quits in from the start!

4. The best strategy in such a flood is to:

   1. Stay still,

   2. Breath slowly and deeply, and

   3. Observe it as it flows around you and past you. Offer no resistance and it will flow quickly away.

If you get in a panic, stay still and watch as it flows past you, around you, through you as you offer no resistance. You will see it subside. This really works and will quickly lead to a reduction both in the intensity of the attack and the frequency of them.

The Balcony Technique

The balcony technique has a special place in my heart. It is a simple and very powerful technique that works every time. I use it whenever I start to feel anxious or fearful. It can be used almost anywhere in seconds - it's that quick.

How to do a Job Interview without the Nerves

Instructions

Before you start I want you to think about a situation that makes you feel anxious. Really feel the anxiety and then read on and see what happens.

Now imagine that you are actually standing behind yourself looking at the back of your head.

As you stand there behind yourself, looking at the back of your head you realise you are actually on a small safe step or balcony looking down at the top of your head.

As you look down at the top of your head you realise that there are a set of glass doors or French windows behind you on the balcony.

You then realise that you are on the other side of the French windows looking through the glass at the back of your head of 'the you' that is standing on the balcony.

As you stand there looking through the glass at the back of the head of 'the you' standing on the balcony you realise there is a huge beautiful ballroom behind you, stretching off into the distance behind you. Notice the beautiful wooden floor and the crystal chandeliers.

You then realise that you are all the way back at the other end of this massive ballroom, looking all the way along the room at the little you looking through the French window.

Then come back to now and notice what happened to the old feelings. They are gone!

This is a really quick way to reduce fears. With a little practice you can do this entire routine in a second or two in your head.

Let the music play

A really powerful way to deal with nerves before the interview is to use music.

I want you to spend a little time constructing a playlist or CD of powerful 'up music'. I am talking about the type of music that when you hear it you start to feel stronger, motivated and alert. Quite often theme tunes like the James Bond Theme or the theme to mission impossible, or any track that gets you going in a positive motivated way.

Once you have your playlist or CD there are a couple of powerful things you can do with it to get rid of nerves:

1. Anytime you start to feel nervous put your 'up tracks' on.
2. On the way to the interview make sure you are playing your up tracks – loudly
3. Find somewhere quiet and sit down with your MP3 / CD player just before going into the interview.

How to do a Job Interview without the Nerves

Movies

Start to construct a movie in your head of the interview whilst playing your up tracks. Make sure that the movie is positive and you can see yourself dealing effortlessly and calmly with the interview. Notice how composed you are and how well you perform.

It must end with you being the hero. Notice how calmly and clearly you speak. Notice how confident you look. Do this as many times as you can before the interview. If, whilst you are playing your movie you see something going wrong, notice how in the movie you deal with this and move on. It is important that you always end the movie as the hero.

How to do a Job Interview without the Nerves

Plans

How to do a Job Interview without the Nerves

A plan for the day of your interview

1. Do not take sugary food or drink fizzy drinks today. Follow the Fear Course 6 golden diet rules.

2. Use your motivational up tracks especially during the morning. Have some great music playing as you are getting ready.

3. Remember your breathing. Practice a few diaphramatic breaths during the morning and use it during the interview and any other time you need it. Remember only a few breaths at a time.

4. Remember your posture. Today of all days, stand up straight. Pull your shoulders back and lift your chin. Walk land sit ike a confident person and you will get interviewed as a confident person.

5. Remember your language and thinking. Change negative certainties into negative possibilities, then into positive possibilities at least. Even better turn them into positive certainties - especially today.

6. Remember your focussed distraction techniques. The chances are you will not need them today but if you have to wait around they may come in handy.

7. Remember the balcony technique. This is a little star of a technique. It is ideal for times like the moment just before you walk into the interview room. It will really help you regain balance and be calm.

8. Use the Positive movie technique I showed you. This is a really good thing to do for a couple of minutes first thing in the morning and then for a minute or two once you are dressed and just before the interview starts.

9. Have a hot milky drink about 30 minutes before setting out for your interview. It will calm you, give your stomach something to do rather than doing back flips and it helps to keep you hydrated.

10. Keep a bottle of water close by so you can have a drink. Drink water often today. It is very easy to forget to drink water and get quite dehydrated.

11. Enjoy the interview! You now have everything you need to have a calm, composed and confident day.

The Fear Course 9 point plan for a calm and composed Job Interview:

In addition to the 10 point plan above here is a plan for the actual interview:

1. Get to the venue in plenty of time. It is far better to find a café and have a drink of fruit juice (not coffee or tea) before the interview than to arrive late or just in time. That way you can listen to your up-tracks and play some positive visualisation movies in your head. You should have practiced this quite a few times and should have some really good positive mental movies by now. Remember if your mind pops up with a problem see yourself dealing with it elegantly and overcoming the problem.
2. When you enter the building where this interview is hold yourself and walk like a confident person. Pull your shoulders back, walk calmly, look up and smile.
3. When you are going into the room where the interview will be, just say to yourself slowly and quietly "Actually I notice I am getting calmer and calmer".
4. When you get to the interview, sit upright in a confident manner. Look up slightly. Do not look down or hunch. This is an absolute must. Your body language not only affects you but also how other people (the interviewers) perceive you.
5. Breathe slowly like I showed you. In through the nose and out through the mouth whilst you are listening.
6. Before you talk take a *slowish* breath in. *Do not* take a quick breath in before you speak. Try both now and notice what happens.
7. *Before* you speak look up and look at the interviewers. Do not under any circumstances start to talk whilst looking down.
8. Take a small pause of 2-3 seconds before you speak or answer a question. Your brain will be operating at 100 miles an hour and the pause is essential, and whilst you may feel like the space is a bit long, I can assure you the interviewers won't notice. In fact someone who answers too quickly does not look like they have thought the answer through. What this pause will do is get your thinking back.
9. Speed is the enemy of good delivery. Go slow, go calm.

Last words

If you've taken the time to read through this booklet and have taken advantage of its strategies, you should be very well-prepared for your job interview in terms of remaining calm and composed is concerned. This should remain regardless of whether it plays out exactly as expected or has to incorporate some impromptu creativity (which can be the case). You've gone through all the challenges and tribulations of getting this far; your interview is certainly something that you can handle, with confidence.

If you employ the basics of anxiety management, have prepared for your interview and any other elements of the interview process, you can face your interview with a clear sense of confidence that these preparations will bring. Your strength during your interview will make all the difference.

Best wishes and good luck for your interview from all the fear course team and myself.

David Wilkinson

How to do a Job Interview without the Nerves

If you would like one-to-one support and even more techniques why don't you try the **Online Fear Course**?

You will get :

- The **entire one day live course** in text, audio and video worth $265
    - 5 Stages, and
    - 29 Individual Step-by-Step Tutorials
    - 7 Major Pathways, including
        - Presentation nerves worth $169
        - Driving test nerves worth $54
        - Fear of flying worth $169
        - Social & dating nerves worth $99
        - Job interview nerves worth $169
        - Download handouts worth $25
        - Online support via online forum $75
        - Voucher for the live fear course $50
        - One Year 'Confidence Course' $80
    - Full support via the VIP forum $200
    - One year Confident Habits Course $175

Go to www.fearcourse.com/ and click 'online'.

References

References

Ahmad, R.H. & Forbes, E.E., (2009) *Genetics of Emotion Regulation*. in J.J. Gross, (Ed) Handbook of Emotion Regulation (pp. 110-134). New York: Guildford Press.

Arce E, et al, (2009) *Association between individual differences in self-reported emotional resilience and the affective perception of neutral faces.* Journal of affective disorders, April 2009, vol./is. 114/1-3(286-93), 1573-2517

Azizi, A. Et al (2010). *The Effectiveness of Emotion Regulation Training and Cognitive Therapy on the Emotional and Addictional Problems of Substance Abusers.* IJoP. 2010;2(5) : 60-65

Banfield, J.F. et al. (2004) *The Cognitive Neuroscience of Self-Regulation*. In R.F. Baumeister & K.D. Vohs (Eds.) Handbook of Self-Regulation (pp. 62-83) New York: Guildford Press.

Beer, J.S., & Lombardo, M.V. (2009) *Insights into Emotion Regulation from Neuropsychology*. in J.J. Gross, (Ed) Handbook of Emotion Regulation (pp. 69 - 86). New York: Guildford Press.

Boss, A.D., & Sims, H.P. Jr, (2008) *Everyone fails!: Using emotion regulation and self-leadership for recovery*, Journal of Managerial Psychology, Vol. 23 Iss: 2, pp.135 - 150

Brandon, J.S. & Baumeister, R.F. (2007) *Self-Regulatory Strength*. In R.F. Baumeister & K.D. Vohs (Eds.) Handbook of Self-Regulation (pp. 84-98) New York: Guildford Press.

Campos, J. J., Frankel, C. B., & Camras, L. (2004). *On the Nature of Emotion Regulation*. Child Development 75 (2): 377-394.

Carver, C.S. (2004) *Self-Regulation of Action and Affect*. In R.F. Baumeister & K.D. Vohs (Eds.) Handbook of Self-Regulation (pp. 13-39) New York: Guildford Press.

Craske, M.G. (2003) *Origins of Phobias and Anxiety Disorders: Why More Women than Men?*. BRAT (Behaviour Research and Therapy) Series in Clinical Psychology. Oxford: Elsevere November 2003.

Davidson, R.J., Fox, A., & Kalin, N.H. (2009) *Neural Bases of Emotion Regulation in Nonhuman Primates and Humans*. in J.J. Gross, (Ed) Handbook of Emotion Regulation (pp. 27-68). New York: Guildford Press.

Dweck, C.S. (2008) Mindset: The New Psychology of Success. New York. Ballantine Books.

Fitzsimmons, G.M. & Bargh, J. A. (2004) *Automatic Self-Regulation*. In R.F. Baumeister & K.D. Vohs (Eds.) Handbook of Self-Regulation (pp. 151-170) New York: Guildford Press.

Gross, J. J. (1998). *The Emerging Field of Emotion Regulation: An Integrative Approach*. Review of General Psychology 2: 271-299.

Gross, J.J., & Thompson, R.A. (2009) *Emotion Regulation: Conceptual Foundations.* in J.J. Gross, (Ed) Handbook of Emotion Regulation (pp. 3-26). New York: Guildford Press.

Kring, A. M., & Werner, K H. (2004). *Emotion Regulation in Psychopathology.* In The Regulation of Emotion, (Eds.) P. Philippot and R. S. Feldman, (pp 359-385). Mahwah, NJ: L. Erlbaum

Larsen, R.J. & Prizmic, Z, (2007) Affect Regulation. In R.F. Baumeister & K.D. Vohs (Eds.) Handbook of Self-Regulation (pp. 40-61) New York: Guildford Press.

Loewenstien, G. (2009) *Affect Regulation and Affective Forecasting.* in J.J. Gross, (Ed) Handbook of Emotion Regulation (pp. 180-203). New York: Guildford Press.

McClure, S.M. Et Al. (2009) Conflict Monitoring in Cognition - Emotion Competition. in J.J. Gross, (Ed) Handbook of Emotion Regulation (pp. 204-228). New York: Guildford Press.

Mischel, W. & Ayduk, O. (2004) Willpower in a Cognitive - Affective Processing System: The Dynamics of Delay of Gratification. In R.F. Baumeister & K.D. Vohs (Eds.) Handbook of Self-Regulation (pp. 99-129) New York: Guildford Press.

Muris, P. & Rachman, S.J. (2007) *Normal and Abnormal Fear and Anxiety in Children and Adolescents.* Oxford; Elsevere. June 2007

Ochsner, K.N., & Gross, J.J. (2009) *The Neural Architecture of Emotional Regulation.* in J.J. Gross, (Ed) Handbook of Emotion Regulation (pp. 87-109). New York: Guildford Press.

Peterson, C. & Park, C. (2009) Explanatory Style and Emotional Regulation. in J.J. Gross, (Ed) Handbook of Emotion Regulation (pp. 159-179). New York: Guildford Press.

Quirk, G.J., (2009) *Prefrontal-Amygdala Interactions in the Regulation of Fear.* in J.J. Gross, (Ed) Handbook of Emotion Regulation (pp. 27 - 46). New York: Guildford Press.

Rothman, A.J., Baldwin, A.S., & Hertel, A.W. (2007) *Self-Regulation and Behaviour Change: Disentangling Behavioural Initiation and Behavioral Mantainance.* In R.F. Baumeister & K.D. Vohs (Eds.) Handbook of Self-Regulation (pp. 1-13) New York: Guildford Press.

Schore, A., (2003). *Affect dysregulation and disorders of the self.* New York: Norton

Tortella-Feliu, M, Et al, (2010) *Relationships between negative affectivity, emotion regulation, anxiety, and depressive symptoms in adolescents as examined through structural equation modeling.* Journal of Anxiety Disorders. April 2010

Vohs, K.D., & Baumeister, R.F. (2007) Understanding Self-Regulation: An Introduction. In R.F. Baumeister & K.D. Vohs (Eds.) Handbook of Self-Regulation (pp. 1-13) New York: Guildford Press.

Wilkinson D.J. (2006) *The Ambiguity Advantage: what great leaders are great at.* London: Palgrave Macmillian.

Zelazo, P.D. & Cunningham, W. A. (2009) *Executive Function: Mechanisms Underlying Emotion Regulation.* in J.J. Gross, (Ed) Handbook of Emotion Regulation (pp. 135-158). New York: Guildford Press.

Printed in Great Britain by
Amazon.co.uk, Ltd.,
Marston Gate.